EDGE BOOKS

THE WORLD'S TOP TENS

THE WORLD'S

MOST DANGEROUS
MACHINES

by Tim O'Shei

Consultant:

Sherry Berghefer

Communications Specialist

Department of Environmental Health and Safety

Iowa State University

Ames, Iowa

34171004480280

Capstone
press®

Mankato, Minnesota

Edge Books are published by Capstone Press,
151 Good Counsel Drive, P.O. Box 669, Mankato, Minnesota 56002.
www.capstonepress.com

Library of Congress Cataloging-in-Publication Data
O'Shei, Tim.
 The world's most dangerous machines / By Tim O'Shei.
 p. cm.—(Edge books. The world's top tens)
 Summary: "Describes 10 of the world's most dangerous machines in a countdown
format"—Provided by publisher.
 Includes bibliographical references and index.
 ISBN-13: 978-0-7368-6439-8 (hardcover)
 ISBN-10: 0-7368-6439-3 (hardcover)
 1. Machinery—Safety measures—Juvenile literature. I. Title. II. World's top tens
(Mankato, Minn.)
TJ166.O74 2007
621.8028'9—dc22   2006003281

Editorial Credits
Angie Kaelberer, editor; Kate Opseth, set designer; PhaseOne, book designer;
 Wanda Winch, photo researcher; Scott Thoms, photo editor

Photo Credits
911 Pictures/Michael Heller, 22, 25, 27 (bottom left and right); Wayne Tomblinson, 24
Corbis/Annie Griffiths Belt, 14, 27 (top left); Kalish/DiMaggio, 20, 27 (middle right)
Getty Images Inc./Stone/Mark Kelley, cover; Stone/Terry Vine, 4
The Image Works/Michael Siluk, 8, 26 (top right)
Peter Arnold, Inc./IFA, 6, 26 (top left)
Photo Researchers, Inc./TRL Ltd., 29
Richard Hamilton Smith, 12, 16, 18, 26 (bottom right), 27 (top right, middle left)
SuperStock/age fotostock, 10, 26 (bottom left)

1 2 3 4 5 6 11 10 09 08 07 06

TABLE OF

CONTENTS

DANGEROUS MACHINES

Portable grinders hurl bits of metal through the air. But these machines weren't quite dangerous enough for our top 10 list.

Machines make people's lives easier. Before the chain saw, people had to cut trees by hand. Without all-terrain vehicles, traveling along a hilly path would be long and tiring. If hydraulic cranes didn't exist, it would be terribly hard to move concrete or steel beams.

Indeed, machines help people perform tasks more quickly and easily. But machines don't always make these tasks safer.

In this book, you will learn about the world's 10 most dangerous machines. All of them were designed to do a job, and they do it well. But make no mistakes with these machines, because one wrong move can have deadly results.

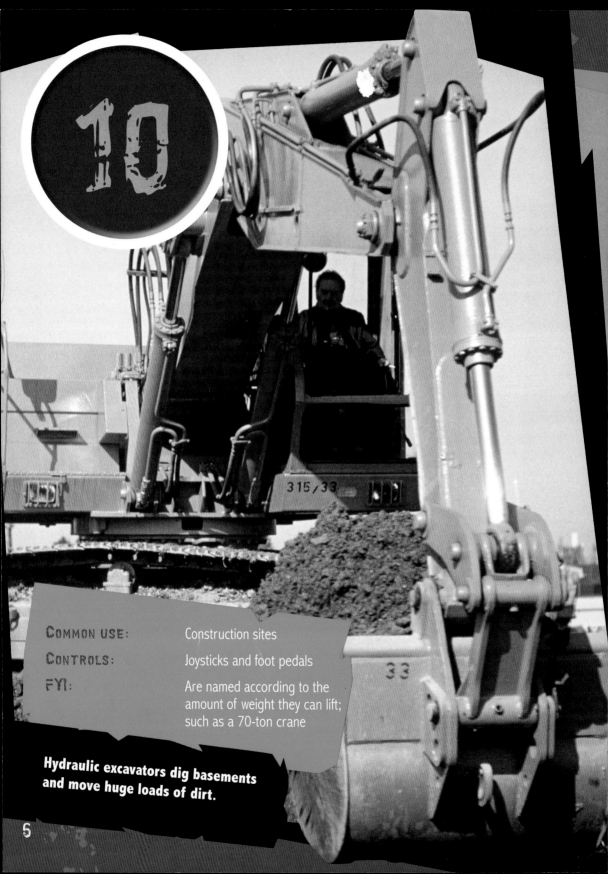

10

315/33

33

COMMON USE: Construction sites

CONTROLS: Joysticks and foot pedals

FYI: Are named according to the amount of weight they can lift; such as a 70-ton crane

Hydraulic excavators dig basements and move huge loads of dirt.

HYDRAULIC MACHINERY

From loads of dirt to enormous machines, hydraulic machinery can lift almost anything. In 1997, a 412,000-pound (187,000-kilogram) train crashed into a creek in Charlotte, North Carolina. Workers used three hydraulic cranes to pull the train from the water and place it back on the tracks.

Hydraulic machines use a system of pistons and fluid to lift hefty weights. The piston system is connected to cables, which move heavy objects up and down.

That's where the danger starts. The heavy objects lifted by the crane can hit people. A steel skyscraper beam swinging through the air is deadly to anyone in its way. Crane operators also have to make sure that they steer clear of power lines. The voltage from the power lines causes sparks that can develop into a raging fire in just seconds.

9

People can reduce lawn mower injuries by wearing safety goggles.

U.S. INJURIES:	About 75,000 each year; 10,000 of these involve kids
SAFETY GEAR:	Long pants, shoes that completely cover the feet, and safety goggles
FYI:	Many injuries happen when people try to clear lawn mower blades by hand.

LAWN MOWER

Anyone who owns a home is likely to have a lawn mower. They certainly are useful machines. A sharp blade can instantly transform a scraggly patch of grass into a cleanly cut lawn. But the same qualities that make a lawn mower useful also make it dangerous.

A swirling lawn mower blade generates a massive amount of energy. It could easily cut off a finger, hand, or foot. Many of the accidental amputations treated by doctors are caused by lawn mowers.

But the danger doesn't end there. When a lawn mower runs over an object left in the grass, disaster can result. A lawn mower can crush an object and spit out the parts at up to 100 miles (161 kilometers) per hour. Shattered glass, nails, and other sharp objects can shoot through the air, puncturing skin and eyes. People can help prevent these injuries by checking and clearing the lawn before beginning to mow. It's time well spent.

8 CHAIN SAW

U.S. INJURIES:	30,000 per year
FYI:	About 10,000 injuries involved hands; another 10,000 were to legs

Chain saw operators should always protect their hands with thick gloves.

Chain saws are probably the most dangerous machine that anybody can buy at a store. No training or license is required to operate a chain saw. But one mistake can cost a person a finger, a foot, or even his or her life.

People commonly use chain saws to cut down unwanted or diseased trees. Firefighters also cut down trees with chain saws to help stop the spread of forest fires.

Even something as seemingly simple as trimming a small tree can be risky. When a running chain saw touches a branch, it sometimes kicks backward. A chain saw can kick back in less than one-tenth of a second, hitting the operator in the face, torso, arms, or legs.

At full speed, the chain revolves around the cutting bar at 45 miles (72 kilometers) per hour. Even the tiniest nick can cause a deep and possibly deadly wound.

An average chain saw injury requires 110 stitches. That makes it an injury worth avoiding.

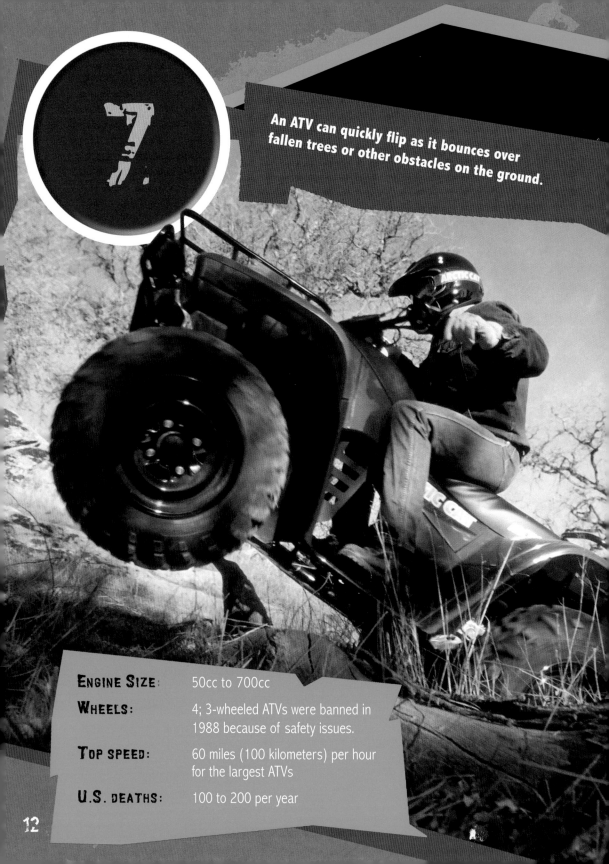

7.

An ATV can quickly flip as it bounces over fallen trees or other obstacles on the ground.

ENGINE SIZE: 50cc to 700cc

WHEELS: 4; 3-wheeled ATVs were banned in 1988 because of safety issues.

TOP SPEED: 60 miles (100 kilometers) per hour for the largest ATVs

U.S. DEATHS: 100 to 200 per year

ATV

From rocks to mud to sand, all-terrain vehicles (ATVs) are designed to cross surfaces that other vehicles cannot. They were developed in Japan, where farmers in the mountains used them to travel.

Americans started using ATVs in the early 1970s. Then and now, ATVs were mostly used for enjoyment. But not everything about ATVs is fun.

ATV drivers have little protection. Unlike a car, an ATV isn't enclosed. The same is true for bicycles, but ATV injuries are 12 times more likely to result in death. Many deaths occur when the ATV goes over bumps. The ATV can then flip over, pinning the rider under the machine.

ATV riders should avoid high speeds, roads with regular traffic, steep hills, large bumps, and any other dangerous territory. Wearing a helmet and taking a rider safety class also help keep fun ATV rides from turning deadly.

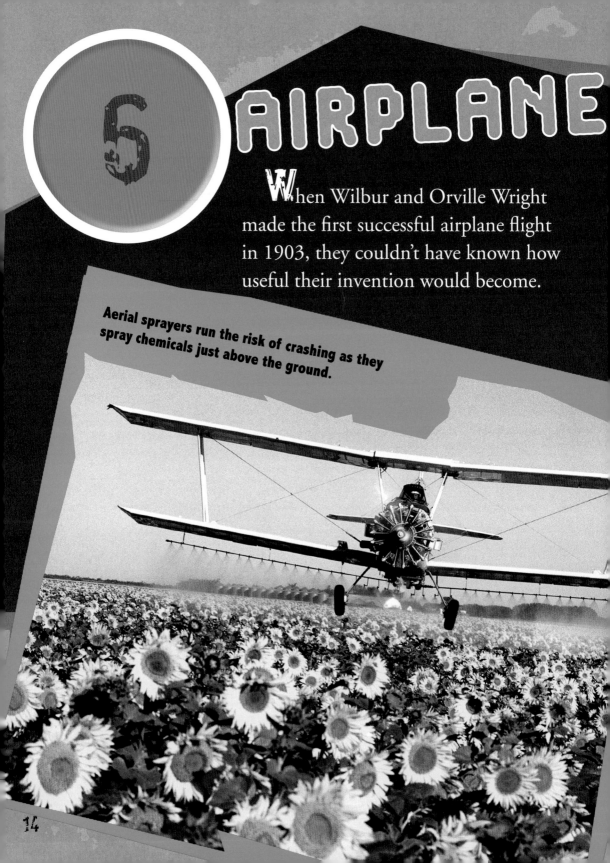

6 AIRPLANE

When Wilbur and Orville Wright made the first successful airplane flight in 1903, they couldn't have known how useful their invention would become.

Aerial sprayers run the risk of crashing as they spray chemicals just above the ground.

Before airplanes, the only way to move people and products long distances involved hours or days in a car, train, or ship. Airplanes make the same trips in a fraction of the time.

Airplanes aren't perfect, though. They can crash, injuring or killing their passengers. Small airplanes that carry only a few people are more likely to crash than larger transport jets. But since transport jets carry many more people, those accidents tend to cause more deaths.

Small airplanes that spray farmers' fields are especially dangerous, mainly because they fly so low. As they swoop just a few feet above the ground, they run the risk of colliding with cell phone towers, telephone poles, or even cars. These pilots must always be alert and aware of their surroundings. Even a second of inattention could cost them or another person their lives.

SPEED:	Large planes—500 to 600 miles (805 to 965 kilometers) per hour; Small planes—100 to 200 miles (161 to 322 kilometers) per hour
U.S. DEATHS:	556 in 2004
FYI:	About 90 percent of registered U.S. planes are small planes.

5 LOGGING EQUIPMENT

Logging workers stay out of the way when a machine loads logs on a truck.

Loggers once chopped down trees using axes and saws. They still do at times, but today, loggers also use machines to do the job.

When loggers mainly cut trees by hand, the work was hard and dangerous. With machines, the work is less tiring and less risky. But blades are still cutting and trees are still falling. About 60 percent of all logging deaths happen when trees, logs, or branches strike or pin workers.

Weather conditions also make the use of logging machines tricky. Machines can get stuck or roll over in snow or mud.

Seat belts and rollover guards on logging machines help prevent injuries. So does protective equipment like helmets, goggles, and steel-toed boots. No logger should enter the woods without them.

LOCATION:	Most logging takes place in western Canada and the northwestern and southeastern United States.
DEATHS:	92 per 100,000 workers in 2004
FYI:	Loggers are 23 times more likely than other workers to die on the job.

4

Farmers must turn off the combine before cleaning out clogged stalks of corn or grain.

AGE: Farm machines are the highest cause of fatal injuries for farm workers less than 14 years old and older than 65.

DEATHS: In 2004, 37.5 per 100,000 workers

FYI: 22,000 kids are injured on farms each year, and about 100 die.

FARM MACHINERY

Peaceful pastures and silently swaying crop fields make farming seem like a safe, relaxing job. It's not.

Farmers work long hours with massive, complicated equipment. Tractors, combines, and other machines can be dangerous, especially after a long day's work.

Tractors are used to pull machinery. They can weigh as much as 40,000 pounds (18,000 kilograms). Imagine what happens when a machine that huge rolls over. Tipped tractors cause most farm machinery-related injuries and deaths.

Combines are used to harvest crops. A long rotating blade in the front gathers soybeans and cotton. Sickle blades cut through stalks of corn and wheat. The kernels or grain are separated and saved. The rest of the stalk is left behind.

Sometimes, stalks can become clogged in the combine, creating one of the most dangerous situations. If a farmer tries to clear the jam without turning off the combine, the blades can start moving. That can result in a lost hand—or much worse.

3

Motorcycle riders must use extra care when passing cars on the highway.

U.S. DEATHS:	3,600 in 2003
U.S. INJURIES:	67,000 in 2003
#1 CAUSE OF DEATH:	Head injuries; wearing a helmet decreases the odds of dying by 37 percent.
FYI:	Colorado, Illinois, and Iowa are the only states without some type of helmet law.

MOTORCYCLE

Motorcycles are fast, stylish, and sporty. They are great fun to ride, particularly in nice weather. They also travel long distances on little fuel.

Motorcycles make for a good ride—if the rider stays on the bike. Unlike cars, which have thousands of pounds of steel protecting the driver, motorcycles are wide open. That is why riders love them, but it is also why they are so dangerous.

Riders who lose control of their bikes can easily be thrown to the pavement or in the path of a passing car. Plus, the small size of motorcycles makes them difficult for other drivers to see. When a motorcycle collides with a car or truck, the motorcycle is almost always the loser.

Motorcycle riders wear helmets and thick leather clothing for protection. Still, accidents can be disastrous. With motorcycles, safe riding is the number one rule.

2

Police officers practice safe shooting at target ranges.

TYPES:	Pistols, shotguns, and rifles
U.S. DEATHS:	About 30,000 each year
BREAKDOWN:	17,000 suicides, 12,000 homicides, 1,000 accidental

GUN

The simple sight of a gun strikes fear in many people. That's why most police officers wear their guns in plain sight, even if they never use them. The gun is a sign of power.

People have guns for self-protection, hunting, and sport shooting. In the hands of criminals, guns are especially deadly. Crime is the main reason why lawmakers have long argued over whether people should be allowed to own guns. In many states, people must pass a background check before they can buy a gun.

Many guns are not available to everyone. One example is the machine gun, which is mainly used by law enforcement and the military. Unlike most weapons, the machine gun doesn't fire only one bullet in a shot. It can shoot hundreds of bullets in a minute. That feature alone makes it one of the world's deadliest machines.

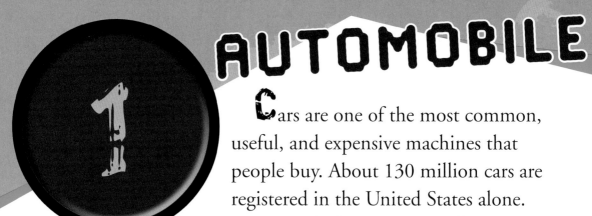

AUTOMOBILE

Cars are one of the most common, useful, and expensive machines that people buy. About 130 million cars are registered in the United States alone. In 2004, there were 6 million auto accidents in the United States.

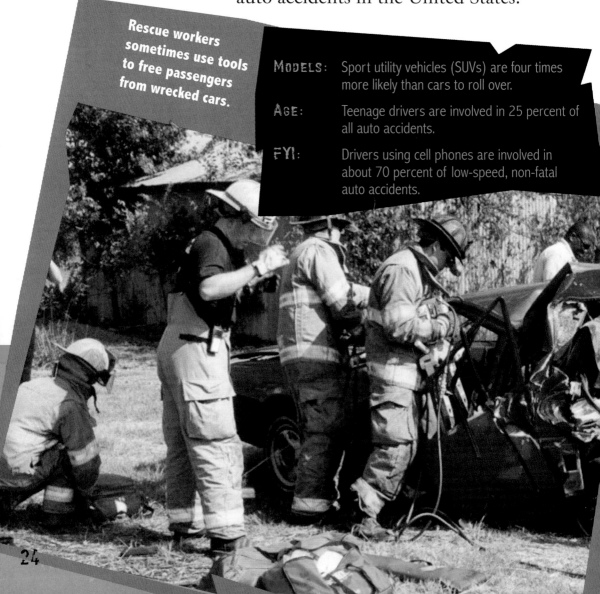

Rescue workers sometimes use tools to free passengers from wrecked cars.

MODELS: Sport utility vehicles (SUVs) are four times more likely than cars to roll over.

AGE: Teenage drivers are involved in 25 percent of all auto accidents.

FYI: Drivers using cell phones are involved in about 70 percent of low-speed, non-fatal auto accidents.

Airbags help save passengers when cars collide with objects.

About 45,000 people died in those accidents. That is enough people to fill a medium-size stadium.

Drunk driving is one of the biggest causes of auto-related deaths. In 2002, about 17,000 Americans died in crashes where alcohol was involved.

Manufacturers have worked hard to make cars safer. Seat belts are designed to hold passengers in place. Airbags provide a cushion for passengers who might otherwise hit the dashboard. But the best safety precaution of all is a careful, alert driver.

THE WORLD'S
MOST DANGEROUS
MACHINES

10

HYDRAULIC
MACHINERY

9

LAWN MOWER

CHAIN SAW

8

ATV

7

AIRPLANE

6

5

LOGGING EQUIPMENT

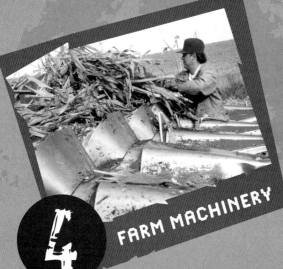

4 FARM MACHINERY

MOTORCYCLE

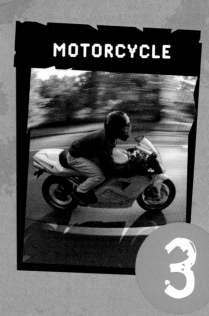

3

2

GUN

AUTOMOBILE

1

UNDERSTANDING MACHINES

Yes, these machines are dangerous. True, they can be deadly. But if people are smart and careful, they can use them safely.

So the next time you see a hydraulic crane at a construction site, don't run. If you see a plane fly overhead, don't duck. When your neighbor is using a chain saw, don't worry. Each of these machines performs a job that needs to be done.

Many of the machines on the list require days or months of training to learn to operate properly. Even using a simple household machine like a lawn mower needs preparation.

Take the time to read the owner's and safety manuals and follow their instructions. If you want to drive an ATV or other recreational vehicle, take a safety class. The time spent learning how to properly operate machines could possibly save your life.

T679413

4P

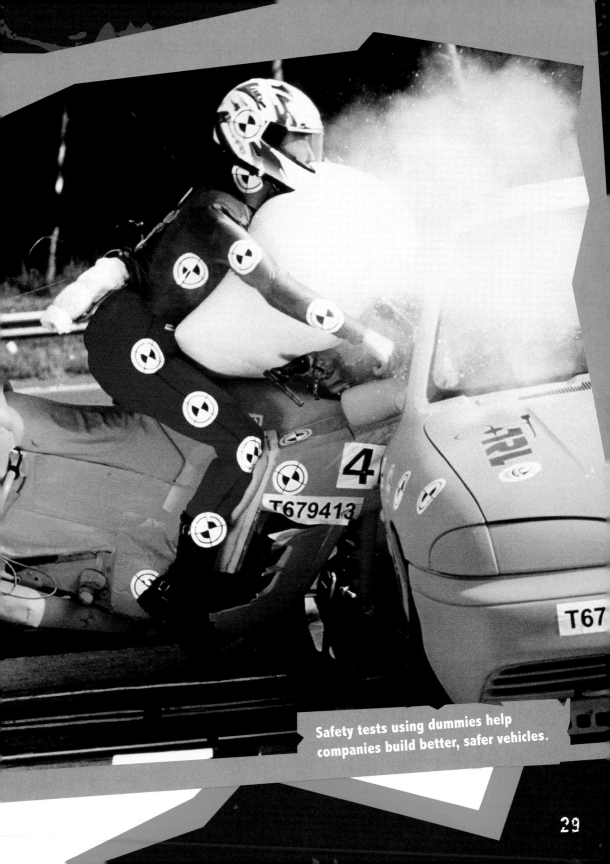

Safety tests using dummies help companies build better, safer vehicles.

GLOSSARY

all-terrain vehicle (AWL-tuh-RAYN VEE-uh-kuhl)—
a vehicle with four large wheels that travels easily over
rough ground; these vehicles are also called ATVs.

cable (KAY-buhl)—a thick wire or rope

combine (KOM-bine)—a machine used to harvest
farm crops

hydraulic (hye-DRAW-lik)—something that works
on power created by liquid being forced under pressure
through pipes

piston (PIS-tuhn)—a part inside a hydraulic machine that
moves up and down, expanding and compressing fluid

Read More

Hirst, Mike. *Monster Machines*. Twenty4Sevens. New York: Tangerine Press, 2005.

Savage, Jeff. *ATVs*. Wild Rides! Mankato, Minn.: Capstone Press, 2004.

Stevens, Ian. *Extreme Machines*. Top 10's. New York: Bearport, 2006.

Internet Sites

FactHound offers a safe, fun way to find Internet sites related to this book. All of the sites on FactHound have been researched by our staff.

Here's how:

1. Visit *www.facthound.com*
2. Choose your grade level.
3. Type in this book ID **0736864393** for age-appropriate sites. You may also browse subjects by clicking on letters, or by clicking on pictures and words.
4. Click on the **Fetch It** button.

FactHound will fetch the best sites for you!

INDEX